The Portable Relaxer

Matthew McKay, Ph.D.,
and Patrick Fanning

MJF BOOKS

NEW YORK

Published by MJF Books
Fine Communications
Two Lincoln Square
60 West 66th Street
New York, NY 10023

The Portable Relaxer
Library of Congress Catalog Card Number #98-65775
ISBN 1-56731-272-1
Copyright © 1997 by Matthew McKay, Ph.D., and Patrick Fanning
This edition published by arrangement with New Harbinger Publications, Inc.
5674 Shattuck Avenue
Oakland, CA 94609

This book was previously published as *The Daily Relaxer*.

10 9 8 7 6 5 4 3 2 1

for Rich Gosse
—M.M.

for Daniel Oberti
—P.F.

Contents

Welcome to the Portable Relaxer

This is a simple book with only one purpose—to help you relax. Open to any page and you'll find a relaxation technique that you can learn in five minutes.

For each technique you'll find a short explanation first, followed by the instructions. The explanation tells you how the technique works, why it works, and what it's particularly good for. The instructions are clear and simple. You should be able to read and understand the technique in a few minutes, and practice it with positive results right away.

The daily relaxers in this book have been distilled from our best-selling *Relaxation & Stress Reduction Workbook,* North America's premier stress-reduction reference. These "best of the best" relaxers have been proven to reduce your physical tension, calm your mind, refresh your spirit, and relieve painful feelings such as anxiety and depression. When you are able to relax at will, you feel better, look better, sleep better, like yourself better, and get along better with those around you.

The Portable Relaxer is easy to use. You don't have to read it all. You don't have to read it in any particular order. Browse until you find an appealing technique. Practice it every day for about a week. Once you've mastered it, you can move on to another technique.

There's enough in here to keep you learning new relaxers for a year, but we predict that in just a few weeks you'll find yourself returning to some favorite techniques that fit your personality and circumstances best. That's fine. Work your favorite relaxers into your daily routine and practice them for as long as you enjoy them. If you eventually get bored with the same two or three techniques, then return to the book for fresh ideas.

If stress overwhelms you and you forget to do your daily relaxers, don't be discouraged. Everybody struggles with stress these days. Just remember that tomorrow is a new day and a new chance to make these daily relaxers part of a permanent lifestyle of stress reduction. Millions of people have been successful with these techniques and you can be successful, too.

Part One

Relax Your Body

Your body is always talking to you. It has a loud voice. It says things like "I'm tense," "I can't breath," or "I don't have enough energy to cope." You can't help listening; and you can't help feeling the tension mount.

The first step towards true relaxation must start with your body. Right now you can change what your body says by spending a few minutes each day giving it a chance to relax.

Body Check-In

How relaxed are you at this moment in time? Where is the tension in your body? If you're like most people, you're probably more aware of your bank balance or the time of day than you are of your own body, even though you're riding around in it. And that's the problem, isn't it? You've been treating your body like a junk car that gets you from one place to another, instead of treating it like a precious temple enshrining your existence.

Your body can actually tell you more about relaxation than any book can. It knows volumes about your unique states of tension and release. All you have to do is turn your attention within, and quietly listen.

Remember to thank your body for keeping you alive and informed, for serving you despite all the times you've ignored its needs. Do something special for your body today: take a bubble bath, get a manicure, use some hand lotion, or wear your most comfortable clothes. Keep checking in with your body. It will tell you truths you need to know, secrets you cannot hear from any other source.

From time to time today, pause in a quiet spot and close your eyes. Allow your breathing to slow and deepen. Ask your body, "Where are you tense?" Scan your body for any tight neck or back muscles, sore joints, tiny aches and pains in your arms or legs, little twitches around your eyes, or places where you are hunched up to protect tender spots.

As you find each twitch, contraction, or distortion, thank your body for showing it to you. Remember that all tension is muscular tension, and all muscle contraction is self-produced, even if you aren't aware of producing it. So, once you become aware of the tension, you can begin to let the tension go. Focus on each area for a moment, exploring the tightness or soreness, even exaggerating it a little if you can. Exhale slowly and allow your tight back muscles to relax, your eyelids to stop twitching, your knees to stop aching. Tell your body, "It's okay, we don't need this tension or this soreness anymore. We can let it go."

Paying Attention

Paying attention to a problem will sometimes solve it. If your son is getting Ds in math and you start paying more attention to his homework, the grade may come up. A spouse who is feeling neglected can be cheered up by more attention. Writing down every cent you spend can curb overspending.

Likewise, tension in your body is a problem that you can start to fix by just paying more attention. When you feel tense or nervous, it's a big help to simply notice and list your physical sensations. For example:

I have a slight headache.

My lower back hurts.

My neck muscles are tight.

I'm breathing in short, shallow breaths.

I feel hot.

Of course, it's difficult to remember in the middle of rush hour or an exam that you're supposed to notice and list your physical sensations. In those situations, you're usually oblivious to your bodily state.

You can improve your chances of remembering to focus on your body and your ability to do it well by practicing this simple exercise in private, when you aren't under stress:

Sit in a comfortable position and close your eyes. Take several deep breaths. Bend your right arm at your elbow, out to the side, and lift the arm so that the tips of your fingers are about even with the top of your head. In other words, raise your hand as though you want to ask a question. Hold it in this position for a while.

As your right arm begins to tire, focus on the sensation of tiredness. Which muscles are actually holding the arm up? Can you find a way to relax them somewhat without letting the arm fall? Scan your body and see if other muscles are tightening. Are your legs tensing because your arm hurts? If so, can you relax them? Focus on your heart, stomach, and lungs. Are you beginning to feel a little anxious? If so, can you find a way to calm yourself? Take several deep breaths and say to yourself gently, "Relax," or "Let go."

After three or four minutes, lower your right arm slowly until it rests in your lap. As you lower it, focus on the sensations. Which muscles are strained and which are not? Can you identify the moment at which the muscles that held up the arm relax? How does the discomfort change? Does it go away as soon as the arm moves? Does it go away gradually? Is there any discomfort as your hand rests on your lap? Can you still feel the muscles you were so aware of when your arm was raised?

Deep Breathing

Deep, abdominal breathing is among the most powerful stress-reduction techniques ever devised. Used properly, it's as effective as Valium and a whole lot faster. It only takes five or six deep breaths to begin reversing a tension spiral. That's because deep breathing stretches and relaxes your diaphragm, the muscle most affected by stress. As your diaphragm relaxes it sends an "all's well" message to your brain, which becomes a signal for your whole body to release tension.

As stress and abdominal tension increase, your breathing becomes shallow and rapid. You breathe mostly in your upper chest. For some people this leads to hyperventilation and the feeling that they can't get enough air. Shallow breathing also changes your blood gasses so the oxygen to carbon dioxide ratio gets out of balance. At best you feel tired, at worst you can get panicked. All this is corrected by slow abdominal breaths that help turn off anxiety by giving you more air.

When you first learn deep, abdominal breathing, it helps to do the exercise lying down. Later you can do it in any posture, virtually any time you need to relax.

Start by putting one hand on your chest, and one on your abdomen (just above your navel). Inhale slowly and deeply through your nose. Try to direct the breath downward into your belly, so it pushes up the hand resting on your abdomen. The hand on your chest shouldn't move much at all. Exhale through your mouth making a quiet whooshing sound.

If you have difficulty breathing into your abdomen, and the hand on your belly doesn't rise, there are several things you can try. Press your hand down on your abdomen as you exhale and then breathe in to push your hand back up. Or, put a phone book on your abdomen at your navel and breathe so that it rises and falls. Another possibility is to lie on your stomach and breathe so that your lower back moves up and down.

If the hand on your chest is rising along with your belly, try pressing with that hand. Direct your breath down and away from the pressure on your chest.

Once you've mastered the deep, abdominal breath, use it any time you feel stress or tension. Take long, slow, deep breaths that raise and lower your abdomen. Breath only when you need to, to avoid hyperventilation. Focus on the sound and feeling of breathing as you become more and more relaxed. Continue deep breathing for two to five minutes.

The Breath of Life

Breath is a necessity of life. Each breath you take is a small miracle of chemistry and physics, yet most people never think about breathing unless the air is polluted or they have asthma or allergies. They take the everyday miracle of breathing for granted.

Take a moment to pay grateful attention to the breath of life:

Like all movement in your body, breathing is powered by a muscle—your diaphragm. The diaphragm is a sheet of muscle that divides your midsection in half, separating your chest from your stomach. Each time you inhale, your diaphragm flexes downward, pushing out your stomach a little and expanding your lungs and chest cavity. When you draw air in through your nose, it is warmed to body temperature, humidified, and partially cleansed.

Your lungs are like an upside-down tree with many branches called *bronchi,* and leaves, called *alveoli.* The alveoli expand like little balloons when air enters your lungs. Each little balloon is surrounded by tiny capillaries—blood vessels that suck in oxygen and expel carbon dioxide with each breath.

All your red blood cells travel through your lungs on every trip around your body. Each time they zip through your lungs they pick up life-giving oxygen and drop off the waste product, carbon dioxide.

When you exhale, your diaphragm relaxes and moves upward, squeezing most of the air out of your lungs, carrying away the carbon dioxide and clearing the way for the next life-sustaining breath of oxygen.

When you're under stress, you tend to tense your stomach muscles, interfering with the full, natural movement of your diaphragm. You may compensate by "chest breathing"—making up for the limited range of diaphragm movement by using your shoulder and chest muscles to expand your rib cage. This is an inefficient way of breathing that further increases your tension.

To become more aware of the beauty and calming aspect of the breath of life, try this breath-counting technique:

Lie down on your back and raise your knees a little to take the strain off your lower back and abdomen. You can close your eyes or just gaze at the ceiling in an unfocused way.

Take slow, deep breaths into your stomach, making it rise and fall with each breath. Don't strain to overfill your lungs—just make them comfortably full.

Pay attention to each part of the breath: the inhale, the turn (the point at which you stop inhaling and start exhaling), the exhale, the pause between breaths, and so on.

When you've developed a smooth rhythm, begin counting your breaths. As you exhale, say, "One." Continue counting on each exhalation up to four. Then begin again with "One." You may become so relaxed that your mind wanders and you lose track. When this happens, start over with "One."

That's all there is to it. This is the simplest possible way to relax. When you are ready to stop breath counting, tell yourself, "I am grateful for the miracle of breathing. I can relax myself this way any time I want."

Out with the New, In with the Old

In 1929, Chicago physician Edmund Jacobson published a little book called *Progressive Relaxation.* His book continues to get attention today: Not many seventy-year-old-self-help books are still in print, let alone still having a major influence. But *Progressive Relaxation* is for three reasons: it's simple, it's easy to learn, and it works.

Jacobson's *Progressive Muscle Relaxation* method is used all over the world as a cornerstone of nearly every relaxation program. It teaches you first to tighten and then relax specific muscle groups throughout your body. In the process, you learn what deep relaxation feels like and how to recognize and quickly release tension anywhere it builds.

The following "short form" of Progressive Muscle Relaxation shows you how to tighten and relax large muscle groups sequentially. Be sure to notice what relaxation feels like in each part of your body. Does it feel heavy? Warm? Tingly? Being able to recognize the difference between relaxation and muscle tension—often so chronic it goes unnoticed—is a key skill.

Remember to tighten each muscle group for seven seconds only, then release.

1. Take a deep breath, way down into your abdomen. As you exhale, let your whole body begin to relax.

2. Curl both fists, tightening forearms, biceps, and pectoral muscles (Charles Atlas pose). Hold for seven seconds and relax. Notice the *feeling* of relaxation in your arms and chest.

3. Wrinkle up your forehead. Hold for seven seconds and relax. At the same time, roll your head clockwise in a complete circle. Then reverse. Notice the *feeling* of relaxation in your forehead.

4. Now make your face like a walnut: simultaneously frown, squint your eyes, pinch your lips, tighten your jaw (unless you have TMJ), and hunch your shoulders. Hold it for seven seconds and relax. Notice how it *feels* when your face and shoulders deeply relax.

5. Gently arch your back and take a deep breath into your chest. Hold the position, as well as your breath, and relax.

6. Take another deep breath, this time pressing your stomach out. Really let it bulge. Hold for seven seconds and relax. Again notice how it *feels* to relax your back and stomach.

7. Now flex your feet and toes. Tighten your buttocks, thigh, and calf muscles. Hold and relax.

8. Lastly, point your toes out (ballerina style) while again tightening buttocks, thighs, and calves. Relax after seven seconds. Notice what your legs feel like when they really relax. Briefly scan your body and allow yourself to feel the relaxation spread from head to toe.

Instant Relaxer

Once you've learned Progressive Muscle Relaxation (see previous section) you're ready for the big league of stress reduction. Soon you'll be able to relax anywhere, any time, with almost instant effectiveness.

Forget Valium. You don't have to wait for that trip to Hawaii. You will soon have a way to relax even in crisis—even if your mother-in-law stops by for an impromptu visit.

The technique, called *Cue-Controlled Relaxation*, hinges on a well-known principle that governs learning: When two unrelated events occur at the same time (for example a chime rings every noon while a monk is saying his prayers) the events become linked in the mind. Eventually, if they occur together often enough, one event can trigger feelings and reactions associated with the other (the mere sound of the noon chime can stimulate peaceful feelings associated with the monk's prayers).

In the next exercise, you'll choose a cue word or phrase that will become linked to feelings of deep relaxation. With a little practice, the mere thought of your cue word, like the monk's chime, will trigger a simultaneous muscle release throughout your entire body.

The first step is to choose your cue word or phrase. Make it something that pleases you, but it also helps if the cue phrase tells you exactly what to do. Here are some examples:

Relax and let go

Breathe and release

Calm and relaxed

Relax now

Peace

You might even choose a favorite color or place as your cue word. Anything will work as long as it is linked, through practice, to feelings of relaxation.

The second step is to relax using the same sequence of muscle groups that you learned for Progressive Muscle Relaxation—but this time don't tighten anything. Just relax each muscle group by deliberately releasing all tension in the area. At the same time, take a deep breath and in your mind, say your cue word or phrase. Here is the sequence:

1. Take a deep breath. Say your cue phrase.
2. Relax your forearms, biceps, and pectoral muscles. Take a deep breath. Say your cue phrase.
3. Relax your forehead. Take a deep breath. Say your cue phrase.
4. Relax your eyes, cheeks, lips, jaw, neck, and shoulders. Take a deep breath. Say your cue phrase.
5. Relax your back and chest. Take a deep breath. Say your cue phrase.
6. Relax your abdomen. Take a deep breath. Say your cue phrase.

7. Relax your calves, thighs, and buttocks. Take a deep breath. Say your cue phrase.

8. Briefly scan your body for any remaining tension. Release it while taking a final deep breath. Say your cue phrase.

Practice Cue-Controlled Relaxation daily for a week. Only when you feel confident in your ability to release tension by willing yourself to relax, should you go on to the final step.

In this step, you relax all muscle groups *simultaneously,* while taking a deep breath and thinking of your cue phrase. You continue to breathe deeply, thinking of the cue phrase with each exhale, and scanning your body for any tightness. Focus on muscles that need to relax and empty them of tension. You should soon be able to achieve significant levels of relaxation in thirty to sixty seconds.

Practice Cue-Controlled Relaxation at first when things are quiet and peaceful. Then begin using your cue phrase in slightly tense situations at home or work. Keep practicing until you can cue relaxation even while your boss looks steamed or your children are fighting in the backseat. And remember, as with any technique, you must invest the time to master this skill. It works!

Visualizing Relaxing Metaphors

Poets know that the way to understanding is through metaphor. "My heart is a soaring hawk" conveys much more than "I feel good." There's something about the human mind that intuitively grasps and prefers metaphorical expression.

What metaphors do you habitually use when you think or talk about stress? Do you describe your cold hands as "ice blocks" or your headache as pounding? Do you think of your sore muscles as tied up in knots?

Metaphors are powerful—they can literally create feelings. For example, you can use metaphorical images of relaxation to visualize tension away. A metaphorical image is any imaginary sense impression that changes, representing the shift from tension to relaxation.

For example, a hot color, like red, could represent tension, and you would change it to a more relaxing color, like blue or green.

Here are some metaphorical images you can use for quick relaxation visualization:

Screeching chalk on a blackboard crumbling into powder

A tight cable or rope going slack

A screaming siren fading to the whisper of a flute

The harsh smell of ammonia or tar becoming perfume or baking bread

A glaring searchlight changing into a candle flame

A dark, confining tunnel giving way to a light, airy meadow

The pounding of a jackhammer changing into the hands of a masseuse kneading your muscles

The following rules for visualizing relaxing metaphors are very simple:

1. Lie down in a quiet place and close your eyes.

2. Scan your body and will your tense muscles to relax.

3. Form mental sense impressions involving all your senses: sight, hearing, smell, touch, and taste. For instance, imagine the sights of a green forest with the trees, blue sky, white clouds, and pine needles underfoot. Then add the sounds of wind in the trees, babbling brooks, and bird song. Include the feel of the ground under your shoes, the warm sun, the smell of pine, and the taste of mountain spring water.

4. Use affirmations in the form of short, positive statements that affirm your ability to relax at will.

The key to making this simple process work wonders is to use metaphorical images when you make up mental sense impressions. So you don't simply see white clouds; you see billowing cotton balls against a faded denim sky.

Autogenic Breathing

Have you noticed how heavy your body can feel when you are deeply relaxed? Psychiatrist Johannes Schultz used that simple fact to develop one of the most effective stress-reduction methods ever conceived. He found that by merely *reimagining* your arms and legs becoming heavy, you could release most of your body's tension and achieve a deep calm. The image of heaviness sends a message to your muscles to relax and let go.

Schultz discovered something else that you may find helpful. When you imagine that your arms and legs are getting warmer—as if, for example, you were lying in the sun—your whole body not only relaxes, but your blood pressure decreases. That's because images of warmth relax the walls of your capillaries and allow your blood to flow with less constriction.

In Autogenic Breathing, you use your imagination to create feelings of warmth and heaviness in your limbs. Let your mind travel to the warm beach, where the weight of the sand gently pressing on your arms and legs calms you and relaxes every muscle in your body.

Begin by taking some slow, deep breaths. Let them go way down into your abdomen. Allow the feeling of relaxation to deepen with each breath.

Now imagine you're at the beach. You can see the seagulls wheeling overhead and you can hear their calls. The waves are rolling up the sand. The surf roars and then grows quiet, rushing in and then receding. Let yourself be lulled by the roar . . . quiet . . . roar of the waves.

Now feel the warm sand. Imagine it pleasantly covering your body. Feel the weight of the sand as it covers your arms and legs. Feel the comfort of its warmth. Warm and heavy. Let the feelings deepen for a while, clearly imagining the sand on your arms and legs. Warm and heavy.

Continue to breathe deeply, finding the relaxation in every breath. Notice the rhythm of your breathing. And as you breathe in, think the word "warm," Really concentrate on feeling the warm sand around your body. As you breathe out, think the word "heavy." Focus on the weight of the sand on your arms and legs.

Continue your deep breathing, thinking, "warm," as you inhale and "heavy," as you exhale. Maintain the image of the beach, feeling your limbs as warm and heavy, for three to five minutes.

Conscious Eating

The best relaxation methods are those that can be woven into the fabric of your daily routine, providing moments of peace and rejuvenation throughout the day or week. The most relaxed people tend to be those who regularly meditate, practice yoga, work out at a gym, jog, garden, paint, and so on.

If you don't have time to devote to a new relaxation practice every day, you can change how you do something you have to do anyway. For example, you can occasionally change how you eat.

Eating delicious, nutritious food in a calm, unhurried atmosphere can be profoundly relaxing. On the other hand, gobbling junk food on the run can add to stress rather than relieve it. Eating while driving, watching TV, talking, or reading can also undermine the naturally calming effect of good food consumed consciously in peace.

The solution is to try to eat one healthy meal or at least one nutritious item a day, taking your time, and concentrating on the food rather than the TV or your schedule.

When you have fifteen minutes to spare and won't be interrupted or rushed on to the next thing, sit down with your food in front of you. For the purpose of this example, we'll assume you're eating an apple. Clear everything out of the way—no books or magazines, no TV or radio, nothing to distract from the food.

First look at the food. Observe the colors and shapes. See the shiny and dull parts of the apple. Next feel the fruit. Hold it in your hand and sense the weight, the slick surface of the skin, the stiff stem. Now smell the apple, taking in the sweet, slightly tart fragrance. Notice if your mouth starts to water.

How do you feel? Give a name to your feelings: *hungry, embarrassed, calm, happy, amused,* or whatever comes up for you. Tell yourself that you accept your feelings as legitimate and all right. Notice any thoughts that you have about this food or doing this exercise: *this is fun, stupid, weird, inspiring; I'm doing it wrong,* and so on. Tell yourself that any thoughts are okay. Remind yourself to approach this experience with an open, empty mind, to focus on the food, and to relax.

Take your first bite. Notice the texture, the snap as the bite comes loose, the taste, the juiciness. Begin to chew slowly and notice how the taste evolves as you continue to chew. Keep track of how your tongue and teeth work together.

Swallow and sense how your muscles work. Imagine where the food is going—to the back of your throat, down your throat, into the top of your stomach. Tell yourself that you are nourishing your body with good food.

Continue to eat, focusing on the physical sensations and tastes. Be aware of your whole body position, your posture, the feelings in your body.

Notice your hunger abating and the sensations of fullness growing. When you feel full and satisfied, stop eating, even if there is still food left. Remind yourself that you often have the option of using mealtimes as a haven of peace and relaxation.

Keep Moving

Your body is designed to move. At the atomic level, all matter can be said to be composed of movement—electrons, neutrons, and photons whiz around each other to make up the atoms, which make up the molecules, which make up everything in the universe. So, you see, everything is in movement all the time. If it stopped, the universe would disappear.

If you stopped completely, you would soon disappear, too. Despite all the movement that goes on inside your body, you still need to move your body on the gross physical plane. If you sit at a desk all day, you'll notice that your body becomes cramped and sluggish. That's because certain parts of your system *require* movement to operate properly.

For example, most people assume that their blood is pumped by their heart. That's true, to a certain extent. But the movement of your legs is also an essential part of your circulatory system. The muscles and blood vessels in your legs are designed to act like a boost pump to get the blood back up to your heart. So, that when you walk or run, your circulation is increased dramatically.

Likewise, your digestion, breathing, and overall muscle tone depend on frequent movement of your body to operate efficiently and stay healthy.

When your job requires you to sit at a desk all day long, you can use the following exercise to keep your body in motion.

Get up out of the chair at least once an hour. Stand up straight with your arms out in front of you.

Swing both your arms upwards and backwards in a slow circle like a windmill. Do this for several rotations. Then do it in the opposite (one forward, the other backwards) direction. Next, try rotating your arms in opposite directions.

Get your legs moving. March in place, lifting your knees high with each step.

Breathe deeply and fully while you're moving. Tell yourself that you are helping your heart by moving your whole body. Rich, freshly oxygenated blood is flooding out from your heart and lungs. It's clearing out the accumulated toxins of inactivity and stimulating your brain to return to work with sharpened faculties.

Part Two

Calm Your Mind

It's possible that you can learn to relax your body, yet still never achieve true calmness. That's because within thirty seconds, stressful thinking can undo the effects of any relaxation exercise. You must learn to live in the moment, by surrendering your anxious thoughts to moments of peaceful reflection and rhythmic breathing. Calming your mind is a necessary step to lasting stress relief.

The Alternating-Your-Breath Ritual

Everyone observes rituals, even the most pragmatic, scientific, skeptical people. You may not practice formal rituals, like the Catholic Mass or Islamic bowing toward Mecca, but you undoubtedly repeat certain small actions that help you get through the day and hold the fabric of your life together.

Some rituals are just habits of convenience, like how you load the dishwasher or arrange your desk. Some are superstitions, like knocking on wood after an overoptimistic statement. Others have talismanic significance known only to you, like the vase in the hall that must have fresh flowers, or the three waggles and a deep breath that must precede every golf swing.

It's good to have a ritual to fall back on when you're under stress and need to relax. You come to associate certain actions and situations as signals to relax: slipping a classical CD into the player, taking your shoes off, loosening your tie, putting your feet up on the desk, lying down flat on your back, and so on. All these simple actions can focus your attention away from external stressors and onto the relaxation process.

Sometimes you can't take off your shoes or lie down. Other times you can get physically comfortable, but your mind still won't calm down and focus on relaxation. In those cases, you can try this alternate breathing ritual, adapted from a Yoga technique. It works well anywhere, anytime, as long as your nose isn't stuffed up. The idea is simple: you breathe first through one nostril, then the other.

There's nothing magic or profound about alternating breath. It just makes you concentrate on your breathing, which is a core method of meditation. It also gives you enough to do with your hand, closing off one nostril and then the other, so that you're distracted from your normal train of thought and forced to focus on one thing at a time. And that's another core idea of meditation. Alternating your breath also helps you relax.

The steps are simple.

1. Sit in a comfortable position with good posture.

2. Rest the index and middle finger of your right hand on your forehead.

3. Close your right nostril with your thumb.

4. Inhale slowly and soundlessly through your left nostril.

5. Close your left nostril with your ring finger and simultaneously open your right nostril by removing your thumb.

6. Exhale slowly and soundlessly and as thoroughly as possible through your right nostril.

7. Inhale through your right nostril.

8. Close your right nostril with your thumb and open your left nostril.

9. Exhale through your left nostril.

10. Repeat for at least five cycles.

Moving Band Meditation

This is an effective and enjoyable combination of imagery, Progressive Muscle Relaxation, and meditation. It is particularly effective because it turns your attention inward and narrows your focus to immediate sensations, like a classic meditation practice. At the same time, the body-based imagery activates your body's natural relaxation response.

Get into a comfortable sitting position and take a deep abdominal breath. Imagine that a three-inch-wide band encircles the top of your head. Try to bring your full attention to the area of your head that's covered by the imaginary band. Be aware of any physical sensations in your forehead. If you notice tension, see if you can release it. Relax away any tightness until your forehead and upper scalp feel completely stress-free.

Lower the imaginary band three inches, so that it covers your nose and mouth. Focus your full attention on the area under the band. Feel everything that's happening in there. Notice what the inside of your nose feels like, your lips, your upper gums, your left ear, your cheeks, the back of your head. Be aware of any tension and release it. Completely relax this area of your head. Take a deep breath as you say to yourself, "Let it go, let it all go."

Just continue to move the band down your body, lowering it three inches at a time (the width of the band). Be aware of all sensations, particularly any tension. As you release the tension, take a deep breath and remind yourself to "let it go." Notice what your muscles feel like as they finally relax.

As the band reaches your torso, imagine that it stretches around one arm, across your upper body, around the other arm, and continues across your back to make a full circle. Try to become fully aware of all sensations in that three-inch area of each arm, your chest, and back. Is there any tension in your shoulders? Your back? Release any tightness you find, and then move the band further down your torso.

Remember to use the phrase "Let it go" as you relax the tension beneath the band. It helps to use the same words again and again—after a while the words themselves will act as a cue to relax.

Continue to move the band in increments down your torso and arms—all the way down to your legs. Notice any tension and release it. Notice the sensation where your legs touch each other, as well as the feeling of your thighs pressing on the chair. Be aware of how your feet feel as they touch the floor.

When the band reaches your feet, let it snap open and disappear. Imagine your whole body emanating a pale blue light. You are deeply relaxed, completely at peace.

Special Place

You need a place where you can escape, where you can be protected from pressure and stress for a while. But sometimes there is no such refuge. That's when you need to create a safe and peaceful place in your imagination, a place you can go any time you need to relax.

Your safe place can be real or fictional. But it should be right for you, an environment where you are comfortable, calm, and beyond the reach of anything that threatens or upsets you. You should go there often, whenever tension starts to build. Merely close your eyes and focus on the image of your special place. See it, hear it, feel it. Even a thirty-second visualization will usually be enough to help you relax.

You can use your special place visualization at your desk at work, just after parking your car, for a moment when your kids are playing with their toys, or any time you can close your eyes for thirty seconds.

Here's how to create your special place: Start by taking a slow, deep breath. Close your eyes and continue to breathe slowly and deeply, letting your whole body relax with each breath. Now let your imagination roam free to look for a special place where you can feel safe and calm and relaxed. It could be indoors or outdoors, a familiar cherished room or an alpine meadow. It could be a place you've been to many times, or a place you've never been to—a place created entirely from imagination.

When you've found your special place, allow yourself to really bring it alive. Notice the view in the distance. Be aware of what's above you and what's under your feet. Notice what's in front of you—the colors and shapes. What do you hear? Whether it's rolling surf, a rippling brook, or a ticking clock, let the sound relax you.

What do you smell? If there is a fragrance, let it be something you associate with peace. Touch something in your special place and notice its texture. Notice the temperature, the feel of the air.

This is your place, and you can have it exactly as you want. If it's too bright or too dark, adjust the light. If it's lonely, add some people. Or if you want to be alone, take them away. Make it warmer or cooler, if you wish. Make it safe. If you need walls or miles of ocean to protect you, if you need a lock or a cliff no one can climb, put them in the scene.

Now imagine you are comfortably sitting or lying in your special place, feeling deeply relaxed. Take a slow breath, way down into your abdomen. Feel your whole body becoming heavy and calm. See what's around you, hear what's around you, feel what's around you. Let it all wash over your senses until you are at peace. Let your special place surround you with its protective grace.

Once you've successfully imagined this safe scene, you can return at any time. Practice shuttling back and forth between your special place and your real environment. Start with your eyes closed for thirty seconds in your special place, then back for a minute to your normal surroundings. Then eyes closed for thirty seconds in your special place, and so on, for five or six complete cycles.

The shuttling exercise will get you to a point where you can enter your special place almost instantly. From then on, it can be a relaxing haven whenever and wherever you need it.

Withdrawal into Blackness

It may surprise you that a lot of stress enters through your eyes. Bright sun or car headlights make you squint. Clashing colors can make you irritable. Sudden movements make you flinch. Wind and dust make your eyes water and blink. Long hours reading make your eyes sore.

Fast-paced TV commercials can exhaust your eyes. The brash ads on signs, billboards, and magazine ads are all brightly competing to grab your attention and hold it. We've created a frenetic modern visual environment that is a continuous assault on eyes that evolved to scan peaceful green and gold savannahs.

There are also emotional stressors that involve the eyes. Urban clutter or household mess—the visual equivalent of noise—can wear you down. Overwork can not only tire your eyes but make you "sick of looking at" your papers. Some days, everywhere you look you see reminders of jobs undone, hopes dashed, obligations unfulfilled, opportunities lost, defeats suffered.

Your eyes are pointed outward because they are your primary tool for observing and comprehending the external world. Your eyes are literally your "lookouts," constantly scanning the horizon for approaching danger or opportunity.

Tired eyes seek blackness as a rest from vigilance and the daily image assault. Blackness shuts you off from the real world and forces you to "look in" on yourself—a physical impossibility and a spiritual necessity.

Try enjoying blackness a couple of times a day. It just takes a minute. Seated at a desk or table, put the heels of your palm directly over your closed eyes. Block out all light without putting too much pressure on your eyelids.

Try to see the color black. You may see other colors, or images, but focus on the color black. Use a mental image to remember the color black: black cats, black holes in space, the back of a dark closet.

Tell yourself you don't have to look at anything right now. Let the muscles around your eyes relax—your eyelids, under your eyes, the crease between your brows, your forehead, your cheeks.

After a minute, slowly lower your hands and gently open your eyes. Remind yourself throughout the day that at almost any moment you can close your eyes and escape into blackness.

Pencil Drop

When localized areas of high-pressure air meet low-pressure air they can spawn a whirlwind that sucks up dirt and trash and moves across the landscape spreading disorder and destruction.

When your high-pressure lifestyle meets a low ebb in your energy level, together they can stir up an emotional whirlwind that makes everything you value—your loved ones, your work, your hopes and dreams—seem like debris swirling around you.

Before you take off across your emotional landscape spreading disorder and destruction, take a moment to relax and center yourself. When your life seems like a whirlwind, the image of the calm center is important. At the exact center of a whirlwind, there is a spot of perfectly calm air.

Tell yourself, "I am the calm center of the whirlwind. I can take a moment to right myself, to return to center. At my core is a calm spot that does not turn with every gust of wind." Paradoxically, when you take your place as the calm center, the whirlwind slows, the dust settles, and your life seems more orderly and manageable.

An ordinary pencil can help you find your calm center. This is something you can do at a desk or table, when you're working on the bills or homework, and you need to return to your calm center quickly and get on with your work.

Pick up a pencil by the point end. Hold it very lightly between your thumb and fingertip, letting the eraser end hang down a couple of inches above the tabletop. Cradle your head in your other hand and get as comfortable as you can.

Close your eyes and consciously slow your breathing. Tell yourself that when you are sufficiently relaxed, the pencil will slip out of your fingers and drop. That will be your sign to let go completely, to just relax and feel peaceful for two minutes.

Imagine you're at the calm center of a whirlwind. You can hear the cold wind whistling, but right where you are it is calm. The sun is shining and you feel warm and secure. Imagine all your cares and worries receding. The whirlwind expands and slows down. The calm center gets larger and more relaxed.

Continue breathing slowly, thinking about calming and relaxing all your tight muscles. If a worry or doubt intrudes, just tell yourself, "That's okay, I can let that go for now and relax. I'll just sit here, calm and centered, deeply, deeply relaxed."

After the pencil drops, continue to enjoy your calm center for a couple of minutes. Then return to what you were doing with renewed energy feeling calm, relaxed, and focused.

Gazing at Special Things

Do you have a special stone, ring, shell, or other small object you've collected and retained? Perhaps there's a certain knickknack that's always on your desk or a coin or pocketknife that you always carry around.

You can use a small special object as an aid to meditation and relaxation. All you have to do is sit and look at it, without describing it in words or thinking about its uses or associations.

There's something about just gazing at a simple object that is relaxing to the human mind. Instead of jumping from one worry or preoccupation to another, your mind can focus on just one subject, and dwell on it without having to make a plan or solve a problem or react in any way. Some meditation masters claim that this is the essence of meditation: the contemplation of one thing at a time, without attachment or analysis.

Have you ever caught yourself staring at a spot on the wall or out the window, thinking about nothing in particular? Explain to your teacher or boss or spouse that you're not goofing off when you do this; you are taking a gazing meditation break, following the ancient pursuit of tranquillity by the detached contemplation of simple forms.

Pick a special thing in your immediate surroundings and use it to practice this gazing meditation. Get in a comfortable position and take several deep breaths. Set your object on a surface that is roughly at eye level, about a foot away from you.

Look at this special thing carefully. Gaze rather than stare at it. Keep your facial muscles relaxed, don't frown or squint at the object.

Notice the object's shape, size, color, and texture. Run your eyes very slowly around its silhouette, as if your eyes were a fingertip slowly tracing the shape.

Next, move your eyes slowly across the object, back and forth, wandering over every inch that is visible to you.

Without using words, describe the object to yourself—try to feel with your eyes its softness or roughness, the sharpness or dullness of its angle, its weight and density. Words and thoughts about the use or meaning of the object will surface in your mind. That's fine. Just notice the thoughts and let them go.

Let yourself become totally immersed in the experience of exploring this object, as if you have never seen it before and it is the most fascinating thing in the universe.

If your body suddenly feels hot or cold or itchy or stiff, notice the physical sensations, then return to gazing at your object.

After five minutes or so, get up and stretch. Notice how much more relaxed and focused you feel.

Changing Colors

How do you feel when you close your eyes and visualize the color red? How do you feel imagining azure blue? Visualizations that use strong, evocative colors often produce a powerful effect. That's because a primitive response to certain colors may be hardwired into your nervous system.

It's been suggested that *red* is associated with tension because it is the color of a forest fire—something that terrified our ancestors. Conversely, *blue* is the color of a cloudless sky. From the beginning of time, that blue said that the forces of nature were calm and we could relax. *White* light encompasses all the colors of the spectrum. For this reason, white light is believed to promote deep peacefulness and healing.

The Tension Cutter exercise uses images of red, blue, and white light to identify areas of tension in your body then release them into feelings of deep relaxation.

Take a deep, slow breath way down into your abdomen. As you continue to breathe deeply, close your eyes. Scan your body from head to toe, noticing the muscles that are tight and the muscles that feel loose and relaxed. You might be aware, for example, that your forehead and neck feel tense, while your stomach seems relaxed.

Now visualize your body as a map or a dark silhouette, lit from the inside by dozens of red (tension) or blue (relaxed) lights. See your clenched jaw blazing red; visualize your loose biceps glowing a sapphire blue.

While continuing your deep breathing, imagine the lights turning from red to blue in all the tension areas of your body. See the red fade as you let go of stress and tension in each of your hot spots. See it replaced by a cool, relaxing blue. Feel yourself growing calmer as the red lights dim and disappear one by one. When the map of your body glows completely blue, experience the peaceful feeling of release.

To further deepen the relaxation, imagine the blue lights glowing a lighter and lighter hue; let them slowly connect up until your whole body is suffused with a calming white or blue-white light.

Going Deeper and Deeper

Self-hypnosis is perhaps the most effective, most pleasurable relaxation technique ever devised; your mind and body begin to feel free, your muscles relax, your attention narrows, and you become more open to suggestion.

You've already been hypnotized many times without knowing it, going into a trance state while driving or daydreaming. Even trying to remember a shopping list or lounging in front of the TV can induce a temporary hypnotic state. You may also have been in a shock-induced trance following a scary experience.

When you learn to hypnotize yourself, you're harnessing a power you already possess: your mind's capacity to disconnect from the pain and pressures of the moment. Hypnosis can offer you a vacation from stress while it refocuses your mind on healing and relaxing imagery.

Before trying the following induction, you'll need to do two things in preparation. First, create an image of a safe and peaceful place. It should be a place that's comfortable and calm, and beyond the reach of anything stressful or threatening. You can use the Special Place exercise on page 32. Second, develop one or two posthypnotic suggestions that will help you stay relaxed when you come back to the real world. Make suggestions for the immediate future (so your subconscious has time to put them into practice). The following list might give you some ideas:

I can awake refreshed and rested.

My body is feeling more and more healthy and strong.

My mind will remain cool and relaxed throughout the day.

Whenever I start to worry, I can take a deep breath and let go.

I feel relaxed, secure, and at ease with myself.

I move calmly and assertively through the world.

1. **Deep Breath.** Start by closing your eyes and taking a slow, deep breath. Take a second deep breath and focus on relaxing your body as you exhale.

2. **Muscle relaxation.** Relax your legs, arms, face, neck, shoulders, chest, and abdomen in that order. As you relax your legs and arms, say to yourself the key phrase, "heavier and heavier, more and more deeply relaxed." As you relax your forehead and cheeks, say the key phrase, "smooth and relaxed, letting go of tension." As you relax your jaw, say the key phrase, "loose and relaxed." Your neck, too, becomes "loose and relaxed." Your shoulders are "relaxed and drooping." You relax your chest, abdomen, and back by taking a deep breath. As you exhale, say the key phrase, "calm and relaxed."

3. **Staircase or path to a special place.** Count each step going down to a peaceful place, and with each step you will become more and more

deeply relaxed. Count slowly backwards from ten to zero. Each number you count is a step going down. Imagine that saying each number and taking each step help you feel more and more deeply relaxed. You can count backwards from ten to zero once, twice, or even three times. Each complete count will deepen your relaxation.

4. **Your special place.** In this place you feel total peace and complete safety. Look around and notice the shapes and colors. Listen to the sounds and smell the fragrances of your special place. Notice the temperature and how your body feels there. If you are at the beach, make sure you can hear the waves crashing and the hiss of foam as the waves recede. See and hear the seagulls overhead. Notice the salty sea breeze, the warmth of the sun on your body, and the feel of the sand beneath you. Try to involve all your senses in building the scene: sight, sound, taste, smell, and touch.

5. **Deepen hypnosis.** Now use the following four key suggestions over and over, in varying orders and combinations, until you feel a deep sense of calm and letting go.

Drifting deeper and deeper, deeper and deeper

Feeling more and more drowsy, peaceful, and calm

Drifting and drowsy, drowsy and drifting

Drifting down, down, down, into total relaxation

6. **Posthypnotic suggestions.** After spending some relaxing time in your special place, give yourself a posthypnotic suggestion. Repeat each suggestion at least three times.

7. **Coming out of hypnosis.** When you're ready to come out of your trance, count back up from one to ten. In between numbers, remind yourself that you are becoming "more and more alert, refreshed, and wide awake." As you reach number nine, tell yourself that your eyes are opening; at ten suggest that you are totally alert and wide awake.

Memorize the basic idea behind each of the seven steps. When you can generally recall each step, you're ready to try your own induction. Imagine your own voice saying each hypnotic suggestion slowly, clearly, and calmly. Take the time to let each suggestion sink in before moving on to the next one. It won't take long before you begin to feel the deep relaxation that hypnosis can give you.

Part Three

Refresh Your Spirit

At our core, we hunger for a feeling of connection—to the earth, to each other, to ourselves, and to our own highest values. When we stop and listen to the voice of our spiritual selves, it always guides us to a place of peace and true belonging.

The Magic Effects of Meditation

Even the simplest meditation experience can affect you profoundly. Just try this for a moment: close your eyes and imagine a candle flame. Tell yourself, "My mind is empty except for the flame. I see only the flame, I think only of the flame." Allow the flame to fill your mind's eye, excluding all other images or thoughts.

Almost immediately, you will think about or visualize something other than the candle flame—worries about an upcoming deadline, plans for a dinner party, hurt over a lost love, anger at your boss—it's just the way the human mind works. Your mind resists emptiness, resists any attempt to focus on a single, feeling-neutral object of contemplation.

When other images, thoughts, and feelings intrude, label them in your mind—"fear . . . memory . . . worry . . . planning" and set them aside. Return to the image of the flame. Remind yourself again to empty your mind of everything but the flame. You may have to refocus on the flame fifty times. Your mind may wander far afield before you remember to bring it back to the flame image.

If you do this meditation five minutes a day for just a week, you'll begin to notice why meditation works. You will start to notice the almost magical effects of repeated meditation, of repeatedly refocusing your mind on something other than what it wants to focus on.

Meditation is a process in which you focus your attention inward, on a single image, sound, or concept. The goal is to achieve a quiet or "empty" mind, free of desire, unattached to past or future. No matter what kind of meditation people do, those who try it eventually come to the same realizations.

- It is impossible to worry, fear, or hate when your mind is thinking about something other than the object of these emotions.

- It isn't necessary to think about everything that pops into your head. You have the ability to choose which thoughts you will think about.

- The seemingly diverse contents of your mind can really fit into a few simple categories, such as grudging thoughts, fearful thoughts, angry thoughts, wanting thoughts, planning thoughts, memories, and so on.

- You act in certain ways because you have certain thoughts that, over your lifetime, have become habitual. Habitual patterns of thought and perception will begin to lose their influence over you once you become aware of them.

- Aside from the thoughts and pictures in your mind, emotion consists entirely of physical sensations in your body. Even the strongest emotions will become manageable if you concentrate on the sensations in your body, and not the content of the thought that produced the emotion.

- Thought and emotion are not permanent. They pass into and out of your body and mind. They need not leave a trace.

- When you are aware of what is happening in the here and now, the extreme highs and extreme lows of your emotional response to life will disappear. You will live life with equanimity.

That "OM" Stuff

Some years ago, a friend attended an all-day meditation workshop, and I was curious about her experience. I first asked about the content of the workshop—what sorts of things she had learned to do. "We just sat around most of the time doing that OM stuff," she said.

It didn't sound very interesting and I almost left it at that. But then I asked how she felt afterwards. "Incredible," she said, "more at peace than I've ever been in my life." And after a moment she added, "I feel like the sea on a calm and windless day."

Her reaction seemed to me a pretty high recommendation for Mantra Meditation—the practice of focusing your mind on a chanted word or syllable. Used for thousands of years throughout the world, this is the most common of all meditation practices. And you can learn the basics in only a few minutes.

Before starting, you'll need to select a word or syllable as your mantra. It could be a word or sound that has personal meaning to you, or it could be nonsense. Some meditators chant a favorite color. Some use the word "one." And many, of course, prefer the traditional mantra, "OM."

Begin your meditation by getting into a comfortable posture. You can sit in a chair, on the floor with legs crossed, or Japanese fashion with your legs folded under you, buttocks resting on your feet. Whatever your position you choose, make sure your back is straight so that the weight of your head falls directly down your spinal column. Rock a little from side-to-side, and then front-to-back to find a point where your upper body feel balanced on your hips.

Now take several deep breaths. Begin chanting silently to yourself your chosen word or syllable. Just keep repeating it over and over in your mind. You'll notice at times that your mind strays. That's fine, but always bring your focus back to the mantra.

Sometimes you'll be aware of sensations in your body. Note them, but then return to focusing on the repetition of your chosen word. Find the rhythm that's right for you, but just keep trying (despite distracting thoughts and sensations) to listen to your mantra.

Now, if you're in a place where it's comfortable, try chanting the mantra aloud. Let the sound of your own voice repeating the chosen word begin to relax you. Keep focusing on and listening to the sound, over and over, monotonous yet peaceful, until you have let go of tension.

Seeking Your Highest Value

In a stressful situation you need to keep your eye on your highest value—the one thing you most want to accomplish, the most important outcome, or the greatest disaster to avoid.

For example, if a heavy workload tends to immobilize you, your highest value might be to "keep moving." If you find getting your kids to clean their rooms frustrating, your highest value might be "Don't lose my temper." If you have trouble finding time to meditate or exercise, your highest value might be "Do it three times a week, no matter what."

If you keep focused on your highest value, you will have won 80 percent of the battle. You might not get everything done at work, but you'll have kept up a steady pace instead of collapsing, and the goal will be in sight. Your kids' rooms might not be cleaned to your entire satisfaction, but at least you'll be on speaking terms with your family. You may not have stripped and waxed the kitchen floor or sorted through all the garage sale stuff, but you can face those leftover tasks with the serenity and positive energy of having met your meditation or exercise goals.

Pick something that has been stressful for you lately: showing up for classes on time, visiting your sick mom, paying your debts, or whatever.

In that situation, what is your highest value? What is the most important factor in coping with your stress? Resist the urge to answer, "The whole thing" or "It's all impossible." If necessary, break the task or situation down into one key part that is important and doable.

For example, perhaps it doesn't matter if you're late for some elective classes, but you really must get to your masters practicum sessions on time. That's the highest value. Or maybe what you hate about visiting your sick mom is all her complaints, so your highest value is not to take what she says personally—to remember that she's frightened and lonely. Or perhaps you can't wipe out all your debts, but you could at least not incur any further debts. You highest value might be to lock up your credit cards.

Take a moment to sit or lie down. Close your eyes and calm your breathing so that it's slow and deep. Imagine that you are in the stressful situation: rushing around getting ready for class, sitting in your mom's hospital room, walking past your favorite clothing or sporting goods store.

See yourself starting to be late, getting upset at your mother, thinking about spending money you don't have.

Then you remember your highest value. See yourself handling the situation so that you preserve your highest value, no matter what. See yourself grabbing a bagel and a sweater and running for the bus on time. Hear yourself saying, "Whatever mom. I'm sure you're right," with detachment and serenity. Imagine yourself remembering that the credit card is home in a drawer and that you don't need any more debts.

Looking Back from the Future

Each separate detail of your life is like a sticky strand of a spider web attaching you to the present. Your attention is fragmented in a thousand directions as you try to keep an eye on the kids, the mortgage, the bills, the appliances, the laundry, the grocery shopping, the cars, the boat, the lawn, the school, the job, the promotion, the raise, the spouse, the trip, the vacation, the parents, the wedding, the funeral, and so on.

It's a full-time job worrying about it all, responding to the sticky tug of every strand of your life. It seems impossible to escape the present situation, to fly out of the web and get some perspective.

But you can escape from the web of the present. You just need to use your imagination.

Just let yourself daydream. Think about the future. But instead of thinking about the near future and whether you can afford a new car next year or what to wear to the Christmas party, think about the far future.

Imagine that you are very old—still healthy and alert, but very old. You've had a long and full life. You are comfortable and secure. You are surrounded by friends and family.

From this perspective, let yourself dimly remember the myriad concerns and worries and doubts that trap you in the web of the present. What will it all matter twenty or thirty or fifty years from now?

When you are old, near the end of a full life, how much will it matter what college your daughter attended? How much will it matter whether you got your teeth capped or moved to a bigger apartment? How much will it matter that your son had a reading problem in third grade? How much will it matter that you had a big fight with your spouse over the credit cards?

Remember that the web that binds you to the present is largely an illusion. Most of the strands are fleeting and ultimately unimportant.

When you imagine looking back from the perspective of old age, focus on the truly important stuff that's going on in your life now. Focus on the love, the hugs and kisses, the quiet moments in the garden.

When you return to your present point of view, try to keep your eye out for those precious moments, and let some of the minor annoyances blow away like cobwebs.

Your Inner Guide

You are the world's leading authority on yourself. You know best what stresses you and what reduces the stress. This inner wisdom is based on a lifetime of living your life from the inside out. It is available to you any time you care to consult it.

The best way to tap into your deepest levels of self-knowledge is to create an Inner Guide—an embodiment of your inner wisdom, an imaginary being who can clarify your feelings and help you understand yourself. Your Inner Guide can take the form of a deceased parent, a long-lost friend or teacher, a character from a novel or movie, or even a symbolic animal like an eagle or a wolf.

You can consciously decide on an Inner Guide, or you can see what kind of guide your subconscious dreams up, as in the following exercise.

One caution before you try this exercise: If at any time you feel uncomfortable or think the guide that is emerging is scary or creepy, stop the exercise and try again later. Wait until you are in a frame of mind that allows you to conjure up a pleasant, warm, supportive, and safe guide.

Close your eyes and imagine hearing a doorbell. Imagine walking slowly and calmly toward the sound of the bell. You approach a large entrance door with a panel of glass in the top half and a screen door on the other side. Through the glass and the screen you dimly see the outline of your guide. Is your guide tall or short? Thin or heavy?

Unlock and open the first door and look at your guide through the screen door. You can see all of your guide, although the backdrop is little dim and shadowy. Look some more and see the details of your guide's appearance. Is it someone you know? Someone you've read about or seen in a movie? Perhaps your guide is a combination of people you have known.

When you are comfortable with your guide, open the screen door and invite your guide to come in and sit down. Smile and see your guide smile back. Shake hands, touch, or hug if that feels right.

Ask your guide, "Are you willing to help me?" and wait for an answer. Your guide may respond with words or gestures, or you may just sense an answer or hear a voice in your head.

Ask your guide, "What is causing my tension?" and see what kind of response you get. Ask, "How can I relax? What can I do to avoid stress?" Accept whatever response is made, without judgment. You may have to imagine your guide several times before you start getting clear answers.

You can consult your guide about any problems you are having, things that are worrying you, decisions you have to make or things in your life that are unclear. You may be surprised at the simplicity and clarity of the replies.

When you are done, say goodbye to your guide and allow him or her to leave. Remember that you can visit with your Inner Guide anytime you need to relax or explore a problem.

Conscious Living

My son loves baseball. When I asked him how he feels up at bat, with the pitcher staring him down, he said, "Kind of relaxed."

"You're kidding," I said, "Your team's rooting for you, people are shouting from the stands, the pitcher's trying to make you look bad—and you're relaxed?"

"When the ball's coming, that's all I see," he told me. "That's the whole world."

I realized then that he had somehow learned a great secret: the art of conscious living.

To understand conscious living you have to start by asking: "How do you relax when you aren't relaxing?" How do you relax if you have to walk six blocks to the store, or drive home on a busy freeway, or wash a pile of dishes after dinner? The answer is to do things with *awareness*—to experience fully the act of walking, driving, or dishwashing.

We generally get into trouble when we try to do more than one thing at a time. Conversely, we experience a basic harmony when our muscles, senses, and thoughts are all working in consort, all focused on the same task. Suppose you're walking to the store while planning how to pay off a loan. The odds are high you won't be having fun. That's mostly because your muscles and senses are responding to one environment, and your mind to another. This division of attention causes stress.

In order to relax, you need to focus your mind on the same task your muscles and senses are engaged in—like my son who thinks only of the ball as all other thoughts and sensations fade. You can learn to harmonize you senses, muscles, and mind when doing these simple everday tasks. The Conscious Living meditations (below) will show you how.

Walking

Walk a little slower than your usual pace, noticing your breath. Say to yourself, "In," with each inhale, and "Out," with each exhale. While continuing to label your breath "in" and "out" try to time your walking so that you start to inhale or exhale at the precise moment one of your feet hits the ground. Get used to this for a few minutes, saying "in" and "out" while getting your steps in sync with your breathing.

Now add one more thing. Count your steps while breathing. Say to yourself "In two, three, four, Out two, three, four." Or the count might be "In two, three, Out two, three," if you're walking slower. Sometimes you'll find that either your in or out breath is a little longer, so your step count will be uneven. "In two, three, four, Out two, three." Your step count may also vary from one breath to the next. That's fine. Just maintain awareness of your breath and the act of walking, keeping as accurate a count as you can.

Driving

Conscious driving requires complete focus on the road. So the first step is to get rid of distractions: turn off the radio, don't drink or smoke, and put away that half-eaten donut. Now give your *full* attention to the act of driving. Be aware of these things:

How far away the car in front of you is

Your speed relative to other cars or the limit

The positions of cars to the side, and cars that are oncoming

The condition of the road

The weather and other driving conditions

Now comes the hard part—keeping your senses, mind, and muscles in harmony. When any thought enters your mind that isn't related to the act of driving, let it pass and gently return your focus to the road. Many thoughts will try to intrude, but you can push them away each time. Try this meditation for three minutes, then notice if you are feeling a little more relaxed at the wheel.

Dishwashing

The key to conscious dishwashing is to focus your full attention on the experience of washing a dish. Try to notice the following:

The warmth of the water

The sensation of wetness on your hands

The hard and slippery surface of the dish

The pressure and effort of scrubbing, the crusts of food dissolving away

The smooth feel of detergent, and the feel of soap bubbles

The act of rinsing away all evidence of soap

Try to keep your mind from wandering from this moment, this experience. For three minutes push away all intruding thoughts—keep your hands, eyes, and *mind* on the dishes.

One with Nature

Why do people find nature so relaxing? Perhaps it's because a return to nature represents a return to humanity's roots, to our primitive ancestry, to an era when we spent all our time out of doors, gathering food, playing, reveling in a simple existence.

Maybe it's true that every life-form on earth helps make up the planetary organism some visionaries call Gaia, and when you immerse yourself in a natural setting, you partake of that larger cosmic identity.

Or maybe time spent in nature reminds us of our childhood, playing innocently outdoors, without an adult care in the world.

It could be that nature simply represents a break from the workaday world, a reminder of vacation time when you can go hiking or swimming instead of dressing up and going to work.

Whatever the reason, the sounds and sights of nature are inherently relaxing. That's why so many relaxation tapes feature soundtracks of waves, wind, and birdsong.

You can take advantage of this automatic association to relax yourself quickly and deeply. Just imagining yourself in a beautiful natural setting is almost as relaxing as going there in person.

You can reunite yourself with nature at any time. You don't have to take time off work, skip classes, travel, or anything. Just take a mental vacation.

Wherever you are, stop what you're doing for a moment and close your eyes. Empty your mind of whatever you have been thinking and worrying about. Replace your worries with the image of a mountain path. Imagine you're walking up the path, near the top of the mountain. Breathe in and out slowly, imagining that you are breathing the clean, tangy mountain air. Smell the scent of pine needles. Feel the pleasantly warm summer sun on your back and shoulders.

Try to sense your muscles swinging you up the trail, effortlessly, painlessly. Feel the earth beneath your feet. Remind yourself that you are a physical being, participating, as your birthright, in the ancient natural history of earth.

Imagine that you come to the top of the mountain. Look around you at range after range of mountains disappearing into the distance on all sides. You are literally on top of the world. Lie down on your back, your spine pressing and merging with the spine of the world. Gaze up into a cloud-dotted sky. Imagine your body melting into the earth, becoming one with nature.

Tell yourself, "I am part of nature. I live and breathe as the world lives and breathes. I can return to my natural roots anytime for refreshment and renewal."

Letting Go of Anger

Anger adds fifty pounds to the load of stress you already feel in your life. It affects your heart and digestion, and increases overall muscle tension. Studies have shown that chronically angry people have higher death rates with respect to virtually every cause.

Anger can affect your relationships because hostile exchanges leave scars. The people you love become wary and less open. The people you work with often withdraw, backbite, or counterattack.

But the greatest cost of anger is to your spiritual self. Anger robs you of a sense of connectedness and belonging to the universe. Instead of feeling joined, empathically, to others, anger alienates you. Instead of feeling inner strength and peace, it leaves you helpless and bitter.

The most important step in freeing yourself from anger is to confront your feelings of helplessness. Anger is about trying to change others, trying to get them to behave differently. When people continue to do what they want, regardless of your needs or beliefs, you feel profoundly powerless. The more you try to change them, the more they resist, and the more helpless you feel. You're caught in a downward spiral that pulls you to deeper and deeper levels of alienation.

You can change the helplessness at the root of anger by using two simple mantras. Say them to yourself each morning, and during every conflict situation.

I cannot control others. Others do what they want.

I am responsible for coping with my own pain. If what I'm doing isn't working, I need to try something else.

These mantras help you to let go of the hope that you can control others. Accepting that others will not change allows you to focus your attention on the one person you can control and change—yourself.

When using the mantras during a time of anger, there's one other important thing to do. Make a plan for change. Think of one specific way that you—without the other person's support or help—can take care of yourself in the situation.

Coping with Anger

Once you've begun to take action and feel less helpless in frustrating situations, you'll have fewer angry interactions. But anger isn't going to disappear. There will still be times of upset when you need crucial coping skills to keep your anger from blowing up.

You can cope successfully with anger by relaxing your body as soon as you become aware of the first signs of anger and by using simple calming thoughts to keep your anger from escalating.

In the first moments of anger arousal, shift your focus to your breathing. Breathe deeply and slowly. With each inhale, say to yourself, "Breathe in." With each exhale, say to yourself, "Relax." Whatever distractions come to mind, return to these words: "Breathe in . . . relax . . . breathe in . . . relax . . . ." Feel each breath bring in peace and calm and send out anger and worry. Notice any tense areas of your body and consciously relax them with each breath.

Now that you're beginning to relax, you'll need a method to method stay that way. The best method is simple self-instruction. Just keep reminding yourself of your basic goals and coping strategies throughout the anger situation. Here are some examples of self instructions that have helped others. You can either choose several that you'd like to try or you can use these as a guide to develop your own self-instructions.

No one is right. No one is wrong. We just have different needs.

No matter what is said, I know I'm a good person.

Just as long as I keep my cool I'm in control.

Just roll with the punches. Don't get bent out of shape.

Stay away from blaming and judgments.

Neutral words only.

Calm and flat voice.

No sarcasm, no attacks.

Getting mad will cost me _____ .
(insert the negative consequences of anger in this situation)

If I start to get mad, I'll just be banging my head against the wall, so I might as well relax.

Getting upset won't help.

It's not worth it to get so angry.

I'm annoyed, but I can keep a lid on it.

I'll stay rational. Anger won't solve anything.

Anger is a signal of what I need to do. It's time to cope.

Don't escalate. Cool it.

There's nothing gained in getting mad.

Easy does it. Remember to keep a sense of humor.

If I'm stuck in a bad situation, I'll think about how to handle this in the future.

Empathy

A wise old proverb says that you cannot understand a man unless you walk a mile in his shoes. But it's not easy to leave your own beliefs, needs, and fears behind, let alone to see the world through the lens of someone else's experience.

This action is a form of surrender, a letting go of self. But it's also as precious as gold, for without it families, tribes, and nations turn against each other. It is a thing called empathy.

Empathy protects us from the corrosive effects of judgment and contempt. It's the antidote for anger. It's the binding force of friendship and marriage. And it is something you can strengthen in yourself with a few minutes of meditation each day.

Sit with your arms and legs resting comfortably. Close your eyes and take several deep breaths. Think the word "peaceful" as you inhale and the word "relaxed" as you exhale. Scan your body for tension and relax any muscles that seem tight. Let your breathing slow as you allow yourself to relax more and more deeply.

Now imagine a chair in front of you. You have negative feelings for the person sitting in it—feelings of anger, disapproval, or hurt. Visualize the face and expression of the person before you; notice how big or small the person is, the clothes, the colors, the posture.

Now make a conscious decision to suspend your judgments and negative thoughts. Take another deep breath and put those judgments aside; for a brief moment just let them go. See the person in front of you as a human being, just like yourself, who is trying to survive and lead a happy life. Meditate briefly on each of these questions:

What needs might influence his or her behavior?

What fears might affect this person?

What beliefs or values are influencing this person?

What lack of knowledge or skills could have an impact on this person's behavior?

What situational limits, problems, or conflicts might be affecting his or her behavior?

And the most important meditation: How is this person sitting across from you doing the best he or she can? How has this person chosen what seems the highest good, given his or her needs, fears, beliefs, and abilities?

Really think about these questions. See the person as struggling to cope, despite fears and longings, limits of knowledge and ability, despite conflicts and problems. Try to see the world through this person's eyes.

Practice this meditation once a day, perhaps after things quiet down in the evening. Each time you do it try to hold the meditation long enough to feel some of your judgments melting away. As anger and judgments dissolve, you are making room in your heart for empathy, even compassion. Notice the difference in the way you feel about that other person—and about yourself.

Part Four

Relieve Your Worry

We are all fortune-tellers, trying to read signs in the present that will help us predict the future. We're forever trying to figure out whether the roof will make it through another winter, whether that look on the boss' face spells trouble, or whether a child's mischief might lead to worse things.

In a sense, our minds are wired for worry. It helps us to survive. But worry has a price of physical stress, illness, and discontent. We need a way to turn it off—to take a vacation from our crystal ball and find joy in the here and now.

Letting Go

Worries and troubling thoughts can to take on a life of their own. There is good reason for this. Through a process called *chaining*, one stressful thought tends to be associated with another, and another, and another—and they're all linked by a common root feeling. Once you open a mental box labeled *worry*, *loss*, or *shame*, all the memories and images in that box come spilling out. Unless you break the chain and stop the thoughts, you may be in for a very hard time.

It's important to remember that thoughts create feelings. Troubling thoughts make you feel more anxious, sad, or ashamed, which in turn triggers more troubling thoughts, more stressful feelings, and so on. You must free yourself from this negative spiral by breaking the chain.

You can let go of worries and troubling thoughts with a simple, peaceful meditation. When the worries subside, so, too, will the tension and anxious feelings. Within three minutes you can start feeling more calm as troubling thoughts drift away like leaves in a stream.

Sit comfortably erect with the weight of your head falling straight down your spinal column. Take a deep breath. Let the air push way down, stretching your diaphragm and relaxing all the tension in your abdomen.

Now imagine a river that is narrow, gurgling over rocks. It's autumn and the trees are aflame, red and orange and yellow. The far bank rises in a steep slope, and beyond it, in shades of gray, are the distant hills and mountains spilling against each other. The river flows to your left, bending after a while out of sight.

A faint morning mist still clings to the trees. Green pines stand tall above the burning autumn colors. You can smell the damp earth on the bank; you can hear the water rippling over rocks. Now your whole body relaxes as you take another deep breath.

This is a place to let go of all troubles, all worries, letting them drift away out of sight. Each time a troubling thought enters your mind, imagine it as an autumn leaf that has fallen into the river. See your worry as a leaf drifting swiftly with the current around a bend and out of sight. As it disappears, take another deep breath way down into your abdomen and feel your whole body relaxing and letting go. Say to yourself, "I am relaxed, I am at peace."

Keep watching the river flowing past you, and the autumn trees on the other bank. Feel the warm air . . . hear the rippling water . . . smell the moist earth at the river's edge. And now, each time a worry or troubling thought comes into your mind, make it a leaf drifting by you, around the bend and out of sight. And as each leaf disappears, take another deep breath, and remind yourself, "I am relaxed, I am at peace."

Panic Control

Have you ever been so scared or panicked that you felt like you couldn't catch your breath? Do you sometimes have moments of anxiety when your heart beats like a trip-hammer, you get flushed, and then weak or shaky? Do you worry about getting so nervous that you'll be too dizzy to stand, or that you'll faint on the spot?

If the answer is yes to any of these questions, then breath-control training is tailor-made for you.

Since any anxiety-provoking situation makes you tense your gut, your diaphragm will naturally tighten, too. That makes it hard to breathe. You compensate by filling your lungs with air and (because your diaphragm is too tight to exhale completely) you end up taking short, fast breaths at the top of your lungs. The rest of your lungs remain filled with the old air you've never completely exhaled.

The result of all this struggling for air is panic—your body goes into a reflexive fight-or-flight mode. Your heart starts to race, you sweat, your capillaries shut down making you feel faint or light-headed, your legs pool with blood (to help you run) and then feel weak and shaky.

It's all normal, but it feels horrible. The solution is to immediately stop the hyperventilation and replace it with relaxing, controlled breaths. Within two to three minutes you'll be much more calm. Try it right now so that the next time you feel anxious, you'll know exactly what to do.

The first step in breath-control training is to stop hyperventilation and panic by exhaling. Empty your lungs immediately and completely. Get rid of all the old air.

Now close your mouth—it's almost impossible to hyperventilate when breathing only through your nose. Mouth breathing, on the other hand, tends to be too rapid and only contributes to hyperventilation.

Put one hand over your abdomen, just above the navel. Breathe in through your nose, slowly counting, "one . . . two . . . three." Try to make the breath push your hand up. Pause a second, and then breathe out, counting, "one . . . two . . . three . . . four." Notice the exhalation is one beat longer. That's because you need to completely empty your lungs on each breath. And it will protect you from taking short, high, panicky breaths.

After you're beginning to feel calmer, try to slow your breathing even further. Breathe in and count "one . . . two . . . three . . . four." Pause a moment and breathe out, "one . . . two . . . three . . . four . . . five." Keep practicing your slow, deep breaths for at least three minutes.

Your Coping Monologue

A coping monologue is a series of positive affirmations you prepare before you have an interview, exam, date, or other stressful situation.

Strange as it sounds, you actually choose and intensify your emotional reactions to any event by your predictions, interpretations, and self-evaluations. If you say to yourself, "I'm going to fail (prediction). I know he wants to get rid of me (interpretation). I'm too nervous and disorganized for this kind of job (self-evaluation)," then your physical response might be sweating, tremors, and a knot in your stomach.

Noticing these physical reactions, you then think, "I'm panicking. I can't do this. I've got to go home." These self-statements increase your physical symptoms and your tendency to make poor decisions. A negative feedback loop is formed and you spiral into a state of chronic stress.

Your thoughts don't have to intensify your fear. You can prepare a coping monologue to act as a tranquilizer for a tense stomach, calming you and pushing away panic. The feedback loop can be a positive one, working for you instead of against you.

When you have a stressful appointment coming up, write down positive self-statements to help you prepare for the situation, confront it, cope with your fear, and reinforce your success. Here are some examples:

Preparation:
I've got nothing to worry about.
Everything will be all right.
I've done this before.

Confrontation:
Just go step by step.
It's okay to make a mistake.
I can do this, I am doing it.

Coping with fear:
Keep breathing deeply.
It will be over soon.
I've survived worse situations than this before.

Reinforcing success:
I did it!
I coped with my fear and succeeded.
I've got to tell somebody about this.

Use these examples as inspiration. The best words for your monologue will be the ones you make up for yourself, in your own words. It helps to write down your favorites on an index card and take the card with you to the performance evaluation, audition, interview, or whatever situation is going to make you nervous.

Changing Channels

Sometimes your mind gets stuck and you can't stop thinking about your back trouble, your bank balance, or your failed love affair. When this happens, your worries make your body tense up, which worsens your negative mental state, which leads to even more tension, and so on, creating a vicious cycle.

When your mind is stuck, it's not enough to physically relax your body. You have to change channels in your mind as well.

But that's not so easy. Has anyone ever told you, "Just don't think about it?" If so, you know how difficult it is not to think about something that's preying on your mind. You need to not only decide to stop thinking about your worries, but also to replace your worries with something else to occupy your mind.

The exercise that follows offers three different ways to change channels. You can change your negative thoughts to positive images, positive actions, or positive affirmations.

When you notice the same old worries haunting your mind, mentally shout, "Stop!" to yourself. Imagine that you hear the word and it startles you into suspending the monotonous chain of rumination that was causing you stress.

As soon as you have interrupted the stressful thinking, replace it with a pleasant daydream. Pick something that you normally daydream or fantasize about—sex, vacation, hobbies, past successes or pleasures, and so on. Pick something you can see yourself doing that is both easy to imagine and pleasant.

If the visualization of a pleasant daydream doesn't work or "wears out" after a while, try swinging into action. Turn on the radio, play a favorite CD, go for a walk, look through your picture album, do some aerobic exercise, pick up a book or magazine, sing a song, or play an instrument. Try to find an activity that is interesting to you and has high "distraction value."

The third method of changing channels is to replace your worrisome thoughts with affirmations. These are short, positive self-statements that you prepare ahead of time. They both distract from and refute negative thoughts.

Affirmations tell you that you are safe, you are okay the way you are, and you can handle any stress that comes along. Here are some examples:

I am well.

I am safe and calm.

I trust my ability to cope.

I am surrounded by support and love.

I can relax my body and my mind.

I can relax now and make plans later.

These are just stomach cramps.

Tests show my heart is strong and healthy.

I can ask for help.

It's okay to say no.

It's normal for couples to quarrel.

This is the same old neck pain, it always passes.

Shutting the Gate

Scientists have identified a specific location in your brain that allows you to focus your attention. It acts as a gate that shuts out competing thoughts and sensations while you zero in on one particular thought or experience. The gate helps you pay attention to a task and stay focused on solving problems. But for some people, especially those prone to worry, the gate gets stuck.

When your attention gets frozen on a particular disturbing thought, it means the gate won't swing shut on the worry so that you can think of something else. Thoughts that stir anxiety and trigger the release of adrenaline are the most difficult to stop. Sometimes, no matter how hard you try to close the gate, it won't budge, and catastrophic thoughts poor into your mind.

The Stop-and-Breathe exercise is like giving a swift kick to the gate so it can finally shut out the anxious thoughts. But interrupting the worries is only half the battle. You'll also learn to give your mind a compelling alternative focus—your own breath.

Whenever you need a break from worries or disturbing thoughts, imagine hearing a voice shout, "Stop!" with sharpness and authority. Give this voice the power of a drill sergeant or the thunder of a great preacher. Make it so loud and so imperative that it can't be ignored. If shouting "Stop!" internally isn't sufficient to interrupt your thoughts, put a rubber band around your wrist and snap it as you shout.

As soon as the flow of thoughts is broken, switch your attention to your breathing. Take slow, deep breaths that expand your abdomen. Place a hand just above your navel and make sure it's rising with each breath. Notice what the air feels like as it passes over your throat and through your bronchial tubes. Notice how it feels to expand your chest and push the air down into your abdomen.

While staying aware of the sensation of breathing, start counting your breaths. As you exhale, count "One," then inhale. As you exhale again, count "Two." Keep counting each exhale until you reach four, and then start over again at one. Keep counting up to four until you feel relaxed.

At the end of the breath counting use a key affirmation such as

I am strong and resourceful.

I am in touch with my peaceful center.

My mind is relaxed.

I can cope with anything that comes.

I'm letting go of all worry.

I can focus on the things I enjoy.

I feel relaxed and serene.

If you use the Stop-and-Breathe method each time a disturbing thought occurs—and you use it immediately, before one thought turns into many—you'll find the frequency of anxious thoughts steadily decreasing.

Setting Goals

Worrying about taking a test or losing your job can be just as stressful as the experiences themselves. That's because your body's primitive fight-or-flight reaction system makes no distinction between imagined experience and real experience. Brooding about danger or loss can make your muscles just as tight and your stomach just as upset as real danger or loss.

When a large percentage of your stress comes from worries about the future, the stress-reduction method of choice is goal-setting and planning.

Think about what bothers you. Look forward to the future and make a mental list of what you worry about most. Is it money? Your relationship? Your kids? Your job?

Pick something you worry about a lot. It can be the most stressful area of your life, or perhaps something of only moderate concern. Use that future worry as a test case for goal-setting and planning.

This is a simple two-step process: set some long-term goals, then plan the short-term steps you need to take to reach the goals.

Close your eyes and imagine yourself five years into the future. Imagine that the problem you've been worrying about is solved to your satisfaction—you have the job you want, the relationship you want, the money you want, or whatever.

What does this positive future look like? Where and with whom are you living? How do you spend your time? Where do you go and what do you do each day? How much money do you have?

When you have this scene clearly in your mind, imagine yourself just one year into the future. Your problem is not totally solved, but it is well on the way to being solved. What has to happen in the next year to get you this far along your path? Do you need to enroll in a course of study, change jobs, ask for a raise, or change how you relate to someone? How does your life look at this intermediate point?

The planning stage now takes over; it's just an extension of this visualization process. Imagine what you need to accomplish by six months from now. Make a list of the applications you have to get in the mail, the information you need to look up, the training you need to begin, and so on.

Then back up to next month and make a list of things to do in the next thirty days.

Then make your list for next week.

Finally, make a short, simple list of things to do tomorrow and resolve to do them. Make sure the list contains small steps that you can actually accomplish.

When you wake up tomorrow, don't start worrying as usual about all the terrible things that will or won't happen five years from now. Instead concentrate on your short list of doable things for the day.

Can't Lose

Do you worry about the future? Do you agonize about conflicts on the horizon? Are you stressed out by the daily hassle of little things going wrong?

If you listen to politicians on the news or read self-improvement business books, you hear about "win-win" solutions to problems. You hear about clever compromises whereby both sides to a conflict get something positive and nobody loses.

Workers get health insurance and management gets higher productivity. Renters get rent control and landlords get tax credits. Teens get midnight basketball and the community gets less graffiti.

But often, the most stressful hassles in life aren't susceptible to the win-win approach. Many situations are just up to chance: It's either going to rain on the day of your daughter's wedding or it's not. You are either going to win the lottery or you're not. Other situations aren't up to chance, but you personally have little power to influence their outcome: Your company is either going to move to Chicago or not. Your son's application to college is either going to be accepted or not.

When you're worrying, hoping, and fretting about these types of situations, you can't negotiate a win-win approach. But you can reduce your stress by adopting a "can't lose" attitude toward the possible outcomes.

The Can't Lose exercise works like this: you say to yourself, "I can't lose because . . ." and you look for the positive benefits of all possible outcomes.

For example, you can't lose because if it doesn't rain, your daughter will have a splendid outdoor wedding, and if it does rain, she'll have a more intimate, cozy indoor affair, more like your own wedding.

You can't lose because if you win the lottery you'll be rich, and if you don't win the lottery you'll be spared the envy of your friends and the greedy attention of strangers.

You can't lose because if your company moves to Chicago you can move with them and have the excitement of a new city to live in (or quit and have the security and familiarity of staying put), and if your company doesn't move to Chicago you won't have your life disrupted.

If your son gets accepted to college out of state, you'll be proud and excited to see him leave the nest and go out into the world. But if he doesn't get accepted and goes instead to the local community college, you will get to hang on to him a little longer.

Is this just positive thinking in advance? Yes. Is it an impossible abandonment of your desire for your preferred outcome? No. You can't really stop wanting what you really want. You'll still prefer winning over losing, sunshine over rain, security over risk, and so on. But if you even half-heartedly try this exercise, you will reap two enormous benefits: First, you'll reduce the present anxiety associated with wishing, hoping, and worrying. Second, you'll reduce the disappointment you feel when you don't get what you want.

Keys to Healthy Thinking

We are what we think. Most of our pain and most of our joy comes from how we interpret the events of our lives. The same promotion can be a vote of confidence to one worker and a load of unwanted stress to another. Faced with the diagnosis of high blood pressure, one person may feel sad and mortal, another may feel anxious, and a third may feel hopeful resolve, taking it as a signal to change diet and exercise patterns.

Epictetus, a Greek philosopher, said it best: "Man is not disturbed by events, but by the view he takes of them." Our thoughts literally create our feelings. Thoughts that focus on danger make us anxious, thoughts about loss make us sad, and thoughts about injustice generate anger. So it's not the promotion that makes us happy or stressed; it's not news of high blood pressure that makes us sad, scared, or resolved. Our feelings about important events are determined by our thoughts, beliefs, and assumptions.

Because thoughts are the womb of feeling, healthy thinking is a prerequisite for a healthy emotional life. Here are five keys to promote healthier thinking in your daily life.[*]

1. **It doesn't do anything to me.** The situation isn't making me sad or scared. It's what I say to myself that makes me depressed or anxious. Changing how I look at things will change how I feel about things.

2. **Everything is exactly the way it should be.** The conditions for people or situations to be otherwise don't exist. They are what they are because of a long series of causal events and preconditions, including peoples fears, needs, reinforcers, assumptions, limited knowledge or skills, past pain, and so on. To say things should be different is to forget causality.

3. **All humans are fallible creatures.** Mistakes are inevitable and un-avoidable. It's crucial that you set reasonable quotas of failure for yourself and others. If you can't accept mistakes, you'll become chronically angry or depressed, depending on who's guilty of the error. The finger of blame will always be pointing somewhere.

4. **The odds for catastrophe are always low.** Anxiety is fueled by unrealistic predictions. What are the odds, realistically, that your plane will crash, that your boss will fire you next week, that the pain in your toe is cancer? Whenever you're scared, try to make an accurate prediction of the odds for catastrophe.

5. **The original cause is lost in antiquity.** It's a waste of energy to try to discover who did what first, or where the problem all began. It works best to refocus your attention on strategies to change the situation now, particularly your own behavior.

*Partially adapted from David Goodman's *Emotional Well-Being Through Rational Behavior Training*.

Changing Bad Feelings

Bad feeling are like bullies—the bigger they are the more and longer you'll hurt. But you have the power to shrink bad feelings to a size that can finally be overcome.

Here is a five-step exercise that will help you diminish bad feelings in stressful situations:

1. Imagine an event or situation that happens often—one that triggers unpleasant feelings. Right now, visualize the scene, also noticing any sounds, smells, or sensations that go along with the image. If other people are involved, notice what they are saying and their tone of voice.

2. As you imagine the situation, notice your reactions. Let yourself feel whatever comes up—anger, depression, helplessness, anxiety, or shame. Don't avoid the feeling. Let it happen. While you're experiencing the emotion, try to give it a name.

3. While still imagining the unpleasant scene and feeling the emotion that goes with it, push yourself to change what you feel. Try to diminish the pain. If you feel anxious, try to change your anxiety to concern; if you're enraged, try to shift it to annoyance; if you feel depressed, try instead to feel disappointment or regret. It may take a few minutes, but you can do it. (Hint: If you're struggling, go back to the previous chapter and recall

how changing your thoughts can change your feelings.) Everyone has this capability. Remember the new, less painful emotion may not last long before you're back to being anxious, depressed, or enraged again. That's okay. The important thing is that you did it—however briefly.

4. Now drop the image. It's time for a moment of self-reflection. How did you downshift the intensity of your emotion? How did you get from rage to annoyance? From feeling worthless to feeling somewhat dissatisfied with yourself? Try to remember what you were saying to yourself while making the feeling less intense. In what small way might you have reinterpreted your behavior or the behavior of others? How might you have seen yourself or others differently in the situation?

5. When you changed your interpretations, assumptions, or view of the imagined situation, however briefly, you also changed the intensity of your feeling. You can change a stressful emotion any time you want by substituting your new ways of thinking. Practice right now by returning to the original stressful image. This time before you get upset, use your new thoughts and interpretations. How do you feel?

Part Five

Improve Your Mood

Sadness is a light that has gone out, the day that is too long. It is the good no longer seen, the dream no longer believed. But sadness, too, can be healed. It can change when you remember your true worth, when you recall the sources of your nourishment and pleasure. It can change, finally, when you learn to protect the one most vulnerable to what you think and do—yourself.

Nourishment from the Past

Memories can be painful—lost loves, moments of embarrassment or fear, times of struggle. But your past can also be a source of strength and inner calm. It's all a matter of knowing where to look, then doing some armchair time travel to reexperience the truly nourishing moments in your life.

The Five-Finger exercise was developed by Dr. David Cheek as a way to achieve deep relaxation and peace, while simultaneously affirming your human worth. The exercise can take less than five minutes. All you have to do is imagine four scenes from your past—using visual, auditory, and kinesthetic (touch) images. It's simple, it's pleasurable, and it works.

Take a deep breath, and as you exhale let your whole body begin to relax. Take another deep breath, and now as you exhale let your eyes close and allow the relaxation to deepen.

Continue to breathe slowly and deeply, counting your breaths on the exhale. Now touch your thumb to your index finger. As the fingers touch, go back to a time when your body felt healthy fatigue. Maybe it was after playing a strenuous sport, or digging in the garden, or hiking a steep trail. Feel how heavy and relaxed your muscles are, feel the warmth and well-being throughout your entire body. Dwell for a minute or two in the scene, enjoying the feeling.

Now touch your thumb to your middle finger. As the fingers touch, go back to a time when you had a loving experience. It might be a warm embrace, an intimate conversation, or a moment of deep sexual connection. Take some time to see, hear, and feel the experience.

Touch your thumb to your ring finger. As the fingers touch, remember one of the nicest compliments you have ever received. Hear it right now; listen carefully. Try to really let it in. By accepting the compliment, you are showing your high regard for the person who said it.

Touch your thumb to your little finger. As the fingers touch, revisit the most beautiful place you have ever been. See the colors and shapes; see the quality of light. Hear the sounds of that beautiful place—the whisper of the wind through the trees or the roar of the waves. Feel that place—the texture, the warmth or coolness. Stay there for a while.

Anchoring

Anchoring is a hypnotic technique that helps you connect to times in your past when you felt truly calm and confident. You can use it right now to give yourself a feeling of strength when facing sad days and difficult challenges.

Right now take a slow, deep breath way down into your abdomen. Let your arms become heavy and relaxed. Imagine them as lead weights and feel gravity pulling them down. Feel your arms sink into a resting place, heavy and relaxed. Your legs, too, can become heavy. Feel them as heavy weights being pulled by gravity, sinking into a comfortable resting place. Keep imagining your legs becoming more and more heavy and relaxed.

Now imagine that your forehead is becoming smooth and relaxed. Your forehead and cheeks are relaxing and letting go of tension. Let your jaw become loose and relaxed. Feel the tension drain away as your mouth opens slightly. Now let your neck and shoulders become loose and relaxed. Feel all the tension easing and letting go. Everything is loose and relaxed.

Take another slow, deep breath, and as you exhale, feel the relaxation spread to your stomach, chest, and back. Feel your whole body letting go of the last bit of muscular tension, releasing and letting go until you are deeply, completely relaxed.

Let a feeling of peace and calm come over you. Feel it wrap around you like a warm blanket. Take another slow, deep breath, and enjoy the sense of warmth and calmness throughout your entire body. Everything is heavy, warm, and deeply relaxed. Each breath makes the feeling stronger. Count your breaths . . . one . . . two . . . three . . . four . . . five . . . six . . . seven . . . eight . . . nine . . . ten . . . letting the warmth and calmness grow with each breath.

Now it's time to imagine a moment in your life when you felt something you really need to feel right now—perhaps it was a moment when you were truly confident. Or a moment right after a success. Or a time when you felt safe and at peace. Or a situation where you felt hopeful and believed in the good times ahead.

Go back to that moment right now. See yourself there. See the confidence or calm expressed in your body. See it in the look on your face. See it in your posture or walk. Hear it in the tone of your voice. Notice how the feeling may reflect in the way others act toward you.

Look inside your body now for that feeling of confidence or calm. Find where it lives inside of you—the exact place. Feel it in the looseness of your shoulders or in your chest. Feel it in your biceps or legs. Experience the confidence or calm of that moment wherever it's expressed inside of you. Take a deep breath and, for a little while, immerse yourself in the feeling.

While seeing, hearing, and feeling yourself in the moment when you were confident or successful, calm or hopeful, gradually move your right hand over your left. Begin to hold your left wrist in your right hand, gently but firmly. This gesture—your right hand holding your left wrist—will be an anchor that can bring you back—whenever you want—to the feelings you have right now. Calm or confidence can be yours each time you hold your left wrist in your right hand and take a deep breath.

Practice your anchor three or four times today until it works quickly and reliably. You'll find it's a great tool for stress relief.

Gratitude

The key to overcoming depression is to recognize how it creates a mental filter that changes your reality. It's like wearing psychological dark glasses that show only your mistakes and the sad, painful things in your life. A lot of the picture is being left out: the experiences and people that you cherish; the moments when you feel relaxed, pleased, or proud; the moments when you laugh and feel part of things.

You may be forgetting the look on someone's face whom you've helped, the warm feeling you experienced when you've been helped, the sigh at the end of the day when you can finally let go and read or watch TV. It's also easy to forget the moments when you were praised, smelled the fresh morning air, or felt deliciously sexual.

Your life has so many things that feel good—even though there's also a lot that hurts and disappoints. You have the power to lift depression's mental filter by actively focusing on all the balancing realities of your life. It takes a deliberate act of will to see the whole picture—the unnoticed pleasures, satisfactions,and sources of contentment, as well as the problems. The I Am Grateful exercise, done at the end of each day, will help you affirm and remember the parts of your life that you truly value and enjoy.

Take a slow, deep breath, and as you exhale, feel your whole body beginning to relax. Notice your legs, feeling them let go of all muscular tension. Say to yourself the words "relax and let go" as you release all tension in your legs.

Now repeat the phrase "relax and let go" as you release the tension in your arms and shoulders. Feel the relaxation deepen as you take another slow breath. Say "relax and let go" as you release all tension in your forehead, cheeks, and jaw. Let your whole face become smooth and relaxed. Say "relax and let go" as you loosen all tension in your neck. Say the phrase one last time, "relax and let go," as you release all tension in your chest, stomach, and back. Take a deep breath, and as you exhale feel your chest, stomach, and back completely relaxing.

Now it's time to reflect back on your day. Let your attention focus on three things for which you feel grateful. It's likely to be nothing major: a warm greeting by a friend or co-worker, a pleasant lunch, a sweet moment with your child, the cool evening air on the drive home, late-night peacefulness in bed. This is your chance to relive and appreciate your experiences, to keep them in mind, to save them from being lost in an endlessly receding stream of time.

Continue to think back on the day. This time let yourself remember three things you did that you feel good about. They'll usually be quite ordinary: perhaps something you finished that went well, something you did to help another person, or a small problem you solved—perhaps even something you did to take care of your health or well-being. For a few moments, let yourself relive these positive events of the day.

Today's Gift of Pleasure

Your time is precious, each moment a potential jewel to be treasured, each hour a unique taste to be savored. Pause each day to notice and enjoy some simple sensations: the laughter of a child, water when you're hot and thirsty, cloud patterns, fall colors. There should always be time to appreciate the gifts of life.

But sometimes it's hard to stop and smell the flowers, isn't it? Especially when the flowers have to be weeded and pruned and fertilized and mulched and watered! The moments fly by, and there aren't enough minutes and hours in the day to accomplish everything that must be done.

Promise yourself right now to take just half a minute today to notice and enjoy something simple in your daily path.

And try organizing your day so you can keep all those moments from flying away.

The next time you make a things-to-do list for your day, write these three words on the paper first: Top Drawer, Middle Drawer, and Bottom Drawer.

Imagine that you have a desk with three drawers. In the top one, you put all the jobs that simply must be done today. In the middle drawer, put all the things that are pretty important, but not as urgent as the top drawer items. In the bottom drawer, put all the stuff that you'd like to get to, but the world wouldn't end if you had to put them off until tomorrow.

Shut the bottom and middle drawers and don't open them until the jobs in the top drawer are done. No cheating! Then do ALL the middle drawer items before moving on to the bottom drawer.

However far you get today, you can rest assured that you have worked on the most important jobs. At the end of the day, congratulate yourself and reorganize your drawers for tomorrow.

Here's a hint: most of the things in the bottom drawer won't be missed if you don't ever get to them.

Treasure Chest

Does your main stress stem from a problem you are trying to solve? Perhaps a chronic health problem, a personality conflict at work, financial troubles, or important decisions waiting to be made? Sometimes the best way to reduce stress is to work on solving the problem that's causing the stress.

It would be nice to have the advice of a very experienced, very wise person who knows you better than anyone else does. But where would you find such a person? Believe it or not, this wise person is you! All you have to do is ask your unconscious mind. Your unconscious remembers everything that ever happened to you: everything that worked and didn't work, every thought and feeling, every person and situation. Not just the stuff that you paid attention to then but have forgotten now, but also the sights, sounds, and feelings you were hardly aware of in the past.

This depth of unconscious information is a rich treasure-house of life wisdom you've stored up and can use to solve problems. The trouble is, the unconscious is just that—not ordinarily accessible to your conscious mind.

Because it's not accessible to ordinary consciousness, you have to tap into your unconscious when you're in a state of extraordinary consciousness—when you're deeply relaxed, in hypnotic trance, or practicing guided imagery, as in the following exercise.

To solve a problem using your own inner wisdom, just close your eyes for five minutes. Try to empty your mind of everything but the problem, as you breathe slower and slower and gradually relax. Contemplate the problem—the person, place, thing, or situation that's bothering you. Let it take center stage in your mind, but stay a little detached. If thoughts such as, "This is hopeless" cross your mind, let them go and continue the calm, detached contemplation of your problem. You're not trying to figure it out, you're just sitting with the problem for a minute.

When the problem is clear, imagine that you are walking along a tropical beach. See the azure waves lapping the pure white sand. Feel the warmth of the sun and the taste of the salt air. Hear the wind in the palm trees that line the beach.

As you walk, you come to a path leading into the jungle. Walk up a gentle rise, under the trees. It's cooler and quieter and dimmer in here. Follow the path upward, following the course of a stream.

Soon you will come to a waterfall. Walk behind the waterfall into a shallow cave. At the back of the cave you find a small treasure chest. The treasure chest contains the solution to your problem. Remind yourself of the problem by letting it enter the back of your mind.

Kneel down and open the chest. Look at the treasure inside. There might be just one object or many things. There might be coins, rings, gems, a photo, or a note on parchment. There might be something you've seen before or something entirely new. Study the treasure you find and wonder how it might symbolize a solution to your problem.

One woman, who was wondering whether to leave her husband, found plane tickets. Another with a back problem found a rose, which she interpreted as "stop more often to smell the roses."

Do this visualization every day for a week and let the symbolic objects offered by your intuitive wisdom suggest a solution to your problem.

Your Assertive Script

We have a friend whose husband is a fanatic for extreme skiing. Nearly every weekend of the winter they're snow camping on some desolate ridge. She either reads or skis cross-country while he climbs further up the mountain for one heart-stopping run. He goes regardless of the weather. On their most recent trip, she had her first case of frostbite.

Our friend likes snow, but yearns to do other things some weekends. And she says that if she never faces another blizzard it'll be too soon.

All of us sometimes endure avoidable stress because we don't ask directly for what we want. We go along with things that irritate, hurt, and bore us. The answer is to learn and use a simple technique for making assertive requests. An assertive request has three parts:

The facts. Here you simply and directly convey the facts of the situation. There's no judgment or negative evaluation of the other person, no pejorative labeling of behavior you don't like. Example: "This is the second time this week you've been late and haven't called." Notice the focus is on straight description. Not judgments like, "You've been late too damn much" or "It's rude to be late and never call." Judgments engender defensive reactions, block listening, and discourage problem solving. Simple facts, on the other hand, leave little to argue with.

What you feel. Here your describe any emotional reaction you may have to the situation using "I statements." I statements are simple reports of your feelings. They don't blame, attack, or accuse the other person. Examples of I statements include: "I feel hurt." "I feel alone." "I feel scared." "I feel sad." Be careful of attacks disguised as I statements: "I feel that you are uncaring." "I feel that you spend too much time at work." These statements are really judgments because the focus is on the other person's faults.

What you want. Here you describe a behavioral change you'd like the other person to make. Be specific. As for exactly what you'd prefer the person do differently. "I'd like you to call if you're going to be more than fifteen minutes late." "I'd like you to supervise Bill's math homework each night." "I'd like you to leave the party with me within thirty minutes of when I say I'm ready to go." Don't ask people to change their attitudes, beliefs, or preferences. It won't work, and they'll resent it. Focus only on a *single* change in what they *do*.

It's time to make a plan. Focus on some of the things people do habitually that increase your stress. Identify person and a situation where you'd be willing to try assertiveness.

It usually helps to script your assertive request in advance. It should have one sentence describing the facts, one sentence acknowledging your feelings, and one sentence requesting a behavior change. Here's an example of how it might sound: "You've been late twice for our appointments this week without calling. I feel a bit hurt, and anxious that we might not be able to get the work done. I'd like you to call me in advance if you're going to be late."

Using the following structure, develop a clear, assertive request:

The facts: _____

_____

What I feel: *I feel* _____

_____

What I want: *I'd like you to* _____

_____

Saying No

Fear of saying "No" is a common source of stress. We learn at an early age from parents and teachers that our right of refusal is not always looked upon favorably.

When "No" drops from our vocabulary we find ourselves stuck with the difficult tasks nobody else wants to do; we feel put upon, sometimes even violated, by the demands of bosses, friends, and family. Other people's needs always seem to come first. It can get to the point where most relationships feel draining—some even suffocating—because we give a lot more than we get back.

Getting good with the *N* word can change all this. The first step is to confront and revise some traditional assumptions about how folks ought to live. The following is a list of values and assumptions that discourage healthy limit setting. Opposite each mistaken assumption is a legitimate human right you should remember as you prepare to say "No."

Mistaken Traditional Assumption	Your Legitimate Right
When someone asks you to do something, it's polite to go along with it.	You have a right to consider your needs and stress level before making a decision.
Saying "No" to people means you aren't generous or caring.	Your first responsibility is to take care of yourself. No one else knows your needs and feelings as you do. Saying "No" means you care about *you*.

It's selfish to put your needs before others' needs.	You have a right to put yourself first sometimes.
People don't want to hear that you feel bad, so keep it to yourself.	You have a right to feel and express pain.
You have to do anything your boss requests of you.	Only you are aware of your schedule and level of stress. It's your right to say "No" when you feel overworked and overwhelmed.
Free speech means people can say anything they want to you.	You have a right to insist that attacking, abusive, or critical remarks stop.
It's impolite to express preferences.	You have a right to your tastes and preferences, and to say when you don't like something.
You should be flexible and adjust; others have good reasons for their actions and it's not polite to question them	You have a right to protest unfair treatment or criticism.
You should always try to accommodate others. If you don't, they won't be there when you need them.	You have a right to say "No" if accommodating costs you too much emotionally or physically.
When someone is in trouble, you should always help.	You have a right not to take responsibility for someone else's problem.

Don't be antisocial. People are going to think you don't like them if you say you'd rather be alone instead of with them.

You have a right to be alone. Even if others would prefer your company, even if they would feel lonely without you.

Right now, scan through the scheduled events of the upcoming week. Make special note of the favors you're doing that you'd prefer to skip, the social contacts that feel more like obligation than pleasure, and the tasks that seem both stressful and unnecessary. Also note upcoming interactions with people who tend to be critical or attacking. Write down these favors, obligations, tasks, and interactions on a chart like the one below.

Now it's time to make a risk assessment. On the chart, note the negative *and* positive outcomes of saying "No" in each of these situations. In other words, try to predict what would happen if you attempted to take care of yourself by saying "No" or setting limits on someone's hurtful behavior. From those situations where the positive outcomes outweigh the negative, choose one where you'll try to set limits this next week.

The last column on the chart is for your plan. How exactly will you beg off, express feelings of being overwhelmed by, or stop the critical remarks? Write your script for setting limits here so you'll have a well-planned response when the time comes.

Event/Situation	Neg. Consequences of Saying "No"	Pos. Consequences of Saying "No"	Plan

Accepting Yourself

What do you have to work with in your life? What are your tendencies? What are your strengths? What interests you? It's terribly stressful and ultimately self-defeating to go against your own grain, to try to make yourself into a totally different person than you naturally are.

If you're shy and tend to make only a few important friends, you will suffer if you want to be more like someone you know who's naturally gregarious and has a lot of casual acquaintances. If you're a hardworking go-getter, you'll probably never have a poet's ability to stop and extract sonnets from the sunset. If you're genetically inclined to be a sedentary, thoughtful, large person, you'll only beat yourself up needlessly by wanting to be like your physically active, high-strung, skinny-as-a-stick cousin.

That's not to say you shouldn't aspire to self-improve. It's just that you need to honestly assess your starting point and accept what you have to work with as basically okay.

So if you have a chronic illness, or you're short, or you don't earn as much money as some people you know—that's okay. It's what you have to work with. The next time your favorite self-deprecating thought crosses your mind, remind yourself to take a break for a little self-acceptance.

The following exercise is a powerful way to quiet internal self-criticism, reestablish contact with your body in the present moment, and raise your self-esteem by simple self-acceptance.

In a quiet moment, just close your eyes and clear your mind of all the negative, obsessive chatter that tends to go on and on. Let it get quiet inside. Let the echoes of your usual monologue die away. If a negative thought surfaces just tell yourself, "It's only a thought" and let it go.

Notice how you're breathing and consciously try to slow it down. See if you can sense your own heartbeat. Listen to the sounds around you. Sense how each part of your body feels: your arms, your legs, your head, your torso.

If you feel a pain, an itch, or a tingle, tell yourself, "That's all right. That's just how it feels right now. I can accept that."

As you feel more and more relaxed, make some positive, self-accepting suggestions to yourself, such as

I accept myself, whatever good or bad happens.

I can let go of the shoulds, doubts, and worries.

I'm only human, I accept my human nature.

I breathe, I feel, I do the best I can.

End your exercise with a promise to yourself to focus on your positive traits and accomplishments.

Matthew McKay, Ph.D., is a founding director of Haight Ashbury Psychological Services and codirector of Brief Therapy Associates in San Francisco. Dr. McKay is co-author of eleven books, including *Self-Esteem, The Relaxation & Stress Reduction Workbook, When Anger Hurts,* and *Couple Skills.* In private practice he specializes in the treatment of anxiety and depression. Dr. McKay is on the faculty of the Wright Institute in Berkeley.

Patrick Fanning is a professional writer in the mental health field. He has co-authored seven self-help books including *Thoughts & Feelings, Messages: The Communication Skills Book, Self-Esteem, Being a Man, Prisoners of Belief,* and *The Addiction Workbook.* He has also authored *Visualization for Change* and *Lifetime Weight Control.*

Other New Harbinger Self-Help Titles

PMS: Women Tell Women How to Control Premenstrual Syndrome, $13.95
Five Weeks to Healing Stress: The Wellness Option, $17.95
Choosing to Live: How to Defeat Suicide Through Cognitive Therapy, $12.95
Why Children Misbehave and What to Do About It, $14.95
Illuminating the Heart, $13.95
When Anger Hurts Your Kids, $12.95
The Addiction Workbook, $17.95
The Mother's Survival Guide to Recover, $12.95
The Chronic Pain Control Workbook, Second Edition, $17.95
Fibromyalgia & Chronic Myofascial Pain Sybndrome, $19.95
Diagnosis and Treatment of Sociopaths, $44.95
Flying Without Fear, $12.95
Kid Cooperation: How to Stop Yelling, Nagging & Pleading and Get Kids to Cooperate, $12.95
The Stop Smoking Workbook: Your Guide to Healthy Quitting, $17.95
Conquering Carpal Tunnel Syndrome and Other Repetitive Strain Injuries, $17.95
The Tao of Conversation, $12.95
Wellness at Work: Building Resilience for Job Stress, $17.95
What Your Doctor Can't Tell You About Cosmetic Surgery, $13.95
An End to Panic: Breakthrough Techniques for Overcoming Panic Disorder, $17.95
On the Clients Path: A Manual for the Practice of Solution-Focused Therapy, $39.95
Living Without Procrastination: How to Stop Postponing Your Life, $12.95
Goodbye Mother, Hello Woman: Reweaving the Daughter Mother Relationship, $14.95
Letting Go of Anger: The 10 Most Common Anger Styles and What to Do About Them, $12.95
Messages: The Communication Skills Workbook, Second Edition, $13.95
Coping With Chronic Fatigue Syndrome: Nine Things You Can Do, $12.95
The Anxiety & Phobia Workbook, Second Edition, $17.95
Thueson's Guide to Over-The-Counter Drugs, $13.95
Natural Women's Health: A Guide to Healthy Living for Women of Any Age, $13.95
I'd Rather Be Married: Finding Your Future Spouse, $13.95
The Relaxation & Stress Reduction Workbook, Fourth Edition, $17.95
Living Without Depression & Manic Depression: A Workbook for Maintaining Mood Stability, $17.95
Belonging: A Guide to Overcoming Loneliness, $13.95
Coping With Schizophrenia: A Guide For Families, $13.95
Visualization for Change, Second Edition, $13.95
Postpartum Survival Guide, $13.95
Angry All The Time: An Emergency Guide to Anger Control, $12.95
Couple Skills: Making Your Relationship Work, $13.95
Handbook of Clinical Psychopharmacology for Therapists, $39.95
The Warrior's Journey Home: Healing Men, Healing the Planet, $13.95
Weight Loss Through Persistence, $13.95
Post-Traumatic Stress Disorder: A Complete Treatment Guide, $39.95
Stepfamily Realities: How to Overcome Difficulties and Have a Happy Family, $13.95

Look for these titles at your local bookstore. Or:

Call toll free, 1-800-748-6273, to order. Have your Visa or Mastercard number ready. Or send a check for the titles you want to New Harbinger Publications, Inc., 5674 Shattuck Ave., Oakland, CA 94609. Include $3.80 for the first book and 75¢ for each additional book, to cover shipping and handling. (California residents please include appropriate sales tax.) Allow four to six weeks for delivery.

Prices subject to change without notice.